Passenger Trains of Yesteryear
Chicago Eastbound

JOSEPH WELSH

KALMBACH
BOOKS

Dedication

To William F. Howes, Jr.

Printed in the United States of America

01 02 03 04 05 06 07 08 09 10 9 8 7 6 5 4 3 2 1

Visit our website at
http://kalmbachbooks.com
Secure online ordering available

Publisher's Cataloging-in-Publication
(Provided by Quality Books, Inc.)

Welsh, Joseph
    Passenger trains of yesteryear : Chicago eastbound /
Joseph Welsh. — 1st ed.
    p. cm. — (Classic trains : the golden years of railroading)
    Includes index.
    ISBN: 0-89024-602-5

    1. Railroads—Illinois—Chicago Region—Passenger
traffic—History.   I. Title.

    HE2583.W45 2001   385'.22'0977311
                    QBI01-201126

Art director: Kristi Ludwig

Maps: John Signor

Cover photo: Niagara No. 6007 rolls out of LaSalle Street Station with train No. 28, the *New England States,* on October 20, 1950. The train operated via Cleveland and Buffalo to Boston. Bob Borcherding photo

Contents

Chicago – Passenger Hub of the Nation

By the end of the nineteenth century, Chicago had earned the title "Railroad Capital of North America." While the city's role as a significant rail terminus was well established by the 1850s, it was in the twentieth century that Chicago actually reached the height of its importance as a railroad passenger hub. The numbers tell the story. During the late 1940s, before the ascendancy of the jet airplane and the interstate, the equivalent of the entire national population—approximately 130 million passengers—arrived or departed Chicago by rail each year. Of these, about 30 percent were intercity travelers while 70 percent were commuters. Before trucks and airplanes stole the business, Chicago's passenger trains also performed a second key role, carrying nearly 7 million tons of vital mail and express annually.

The majority of intercity passengers terminated or originated in the "Windy City," while a healthy minority continued their journey by connecting to other trains there. For a brief period between 1946 and 1958, "through" passenger cars, exchanged between the railroads, were employed to make the transfer easy. Before and after that, passengers were obliged to connect between trains and frequently between stations. They typically used a Chicago institution—the Parmelee Transfer Company (established in 1853) and its successor Railroad Transfer to make their connections. For those with time on their hands, the interval between trains was often spent getting acquainted, or reacquainted, with one of America's great cities.

Handling the number of passengers Chicago received in the 1940s required a massive effort. On average, a passenger train arrived or departed the city every 51 seconds. Influenced heavily by the commuter rush, mornings and evenings were particularly busy. Ten passenger trains arrived or departed every minute in the a.m. peak. The process repeated itself in the evening rush, when an average of 12 passenger trains arrived or departed the city every 60 seconds.

With a host of trains and facilities and more than 7,000 track miles compressed into a 200-square-mile area, Chicago was the biggest and busiest railroad hub in the nation. Passenger trains originated and terminated at six major intercity railroad terminals or a handful of other commuter and interurban stations. To get there, they traveled over a spider's web of track on 23 different railroads forming a series of famous junctions such as 21st Street, Englewood, or Western Avenue. More than 3,600 passenger cars could be found stored in Chicago's far-flung coach yards every day.

Trains to the East and South

Like their passengers, Chicago's trains to and from the east ranged from celebrity to commoner. Some of the greatest trains in the world called Chicago home. New York Central's *20th Century Limited* to New York justly proclaimed itself the "Most Famous Train in the World." In the pre-jet era, movie stars and newsmakers frequented it, and the press staked out the train's Chicago terminal, LaSalle Street Station, every day in search of a radio interview or a few inches of news copy. A worthy competitor to the *Century* was the Pennsylvania Railroad's patrician *Broadway Limited* (established in 1902) to Philadelphia and New York. To Washington, D.C., the unquestioned leader was the Baltimore & Ohio's exquisite all-Pullman *Capitol Limited.* Illinois Central offered the outstanding *Panama Limited* to New Orleans. Its sparkling clean exterior and outstanding cuisine underscored the railroad's pride in the train. Famous Florida trains like the *Dixie Flyer* attracted those longing to escape Chicago's harsh winter weather.

But the majority of Chicago's trains were lesser known. Passengers traveling on the workaday *Erie Limited* or *Nickel Plate Limited* to upstate New York were unlikely to make headlines. Chicago & Eastern Illinois' obscure *Meadowlark* terminated at Cypress, Ill., a town with a population of only 300. The quaint Monon linked quiet downstate Indiana to Chicago. Dozens of other trains, some distinguished only by their train numbers in the *Official Guide,* faithfully operated day in and day out.

Unremarkable but ever present, hundreds of commuter trains trundled over Chicago's rails on their daily mission. On lines stretching south of the city, Illinois Central's massive fleet of electric cars handled more of Chicago's commuters on more trains than any other railroad. To a lesser degree, the New York

Central, Pennsylvania, and Chicago & Western Indiana Railroad offered limited commuter services east and south of the city.

Streamliners Burst onto the Scene

As streamlining came into vogue in the 1930s and '40s, Chicago hosted the sleek new trains in record numbers. The Illinois Central's *Green Diamond,* introduced in May 1936, was advertised as the first standard-size diesel streamliner in the nation. The modernized *20th Century Limited* and *Broadway Limited* of 1938 were touted as the first all-room streamliners in America. In the wake of the Great Depression, the all-coach streamliner grew in popularity among budget-minded travelers. PRR's Trail Blazer and NYC's Pacemaker pioneered the way on the eastern lines. In 1940 three coach lightweight trains (Illinois Central's *City of Miami,* PRR's *South Wind,* and C&EI's *Dixie Flagler*) were intro-duced. They began an immensely popular service, operating over a total of nine railroads to link Chicago with Miami. Last but not least, Illinois Central streamlined its elegant Panama Limited in 1942.

But then came World War II and with it a temporary end to the delivery of new lightweight trains.

Streamlining returned with a vengeance after the war. By the early 1950s, dozens of streamliners linked Chicago to every major population center east and south. Railroads offered competing streamliners in several markets. But despite the popularity of the new trains, some of Chicago's trains remained heavy-weight affairs into the 1960s.

The Diesel Revolution

Like streamlining, the diesel loco-motive promised to revolutionize railroading. Chicago hosted its first regularly scheduled diesel-powered train on roads to the east and south in 1936 when the Illinois Central's *Green Diamond* debuted featuring a diesel-powered cab car. By 1937, Electro Motive Corp. had introduced the very first version of its stream-lined E-series passenger locomotive at the head end of the Baltimore & Ohio's *Capitol Limited.*

Rising to the challenge, steam refused to cede the market. New York Central's streamlined J-class Hudson locomotives, styled by famed industrial designer Henry Dreyfuss, hauled the 1938 *20th Century Limited.* The locomotives would become the very symbol of the streamlined era. Handsome stream-lined K4s locomotives would occa-sionally haul the Pennsylvania Rail-road's *Broadway Limited or South Wind.* PRR's radical new T1 and its experimental S1, styled by designer Raymond Loewy, also came to call. C&EI's *Dixie Flagler* was also pulled by streamlined steam. While their more-glamorous counterparts got all the publicity, hundreds of unstreamlined steam locomotives continued to do their job with little fanfare.

But steam was on its way out. Thanks to lower operating costs and higher reliability, internal combustion expanded its influence and eclipsed the steam locomotive rapidly. Chicago became home to the seemingly omnipresent E and F unit passenger diesels as well as oddities like the American Locomotive Company (Alco) DL-109, the Baldwin "Centipede," and the Fairbanks-Morse "Erie-Built," as well as the beautiful Alco PA.

Sadly, the fascinating transition period of proud steam locomotives puffing out their last miles side by side with sleek new diesels and shiny streamliners was all too brief.

In 1957 Grand Trunk Western operated the last regularly scheduled steam-powered passenger train into Chicago. By the 1960s, the privately operated intercity passenger train itself, reeling from auto and airliner competition, was in precipitous decline. As the strongest rail hub in the country, Chicago hosted the best of the holdouts. The *20th Century Limited* lost its all-Pullman status in 1958, but the *Broadway Limited* and the *Panama Limited* hung on into the 1960s as two of the last exclusively first-class trains in America. IC's *City of New Orleans* also remained incredibly popular. Unfortunately, these beautiful trains alone couldn't overcome the financial deficits the railroads were experiencing.

End of an Era

In May 1971, the quasi-public entity Amtrak was founded to operate intercity rail services and relieve the railroads of the financial burden of the passenger train. Today, Chicago remains and the focal point of Amtrak's national system. But, alas, the trains carry a nearly uniform paint scheme and are powered by a mere handful of different types of locomotives. Chicago's commuter trains, now publicly funded, are more important than ever, given the area's growth and traffic congestion. But charming steam locomotives or first-generation diesels no longer power them.

Despite Chicago's continued importance as a rail hub, its finest days were the fascinating decades of the thirties, forties, and fifties. With its unprecedented volume and variety, Chicago in that era was, arguably, the best place in the world at the best time in history to watch passenger trains. In the following pages you'll learn why.

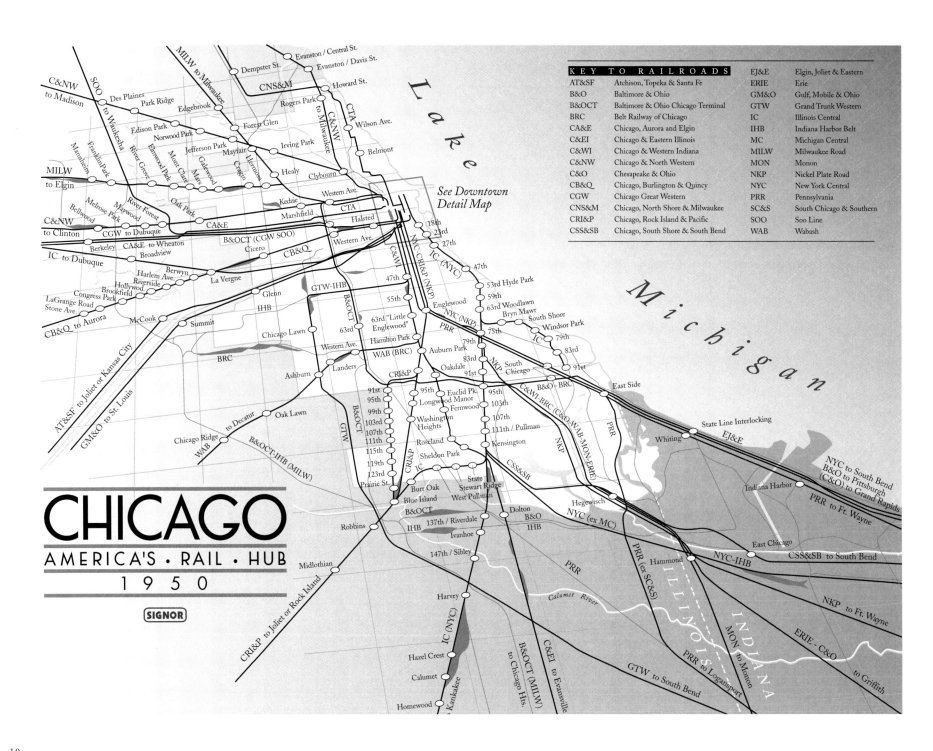

CHICAGO
AMERICA'S · RAIL · HUB
1950

SIGNOR

KEY TO RAILROADS

AT&SF	Atchison, Topeka & Santa Fe		EJ&E	Elgin, Joliet & Eastern
B&O	Baltimore & Ohio		ERIE	Erie
B&OCT	Baltimore & Ohio Chicago Terminal		GM&O	Gulf, Mobile & Ohio
BRC	Belt Railway of Chicago		GTW	Grand Trunk Western
CA&E	Chicago, Aurora and Elgin		IC	Illinois Central
C&EI	Chicago & Eastern Illinois		IHB	Indiana Harbor Belt
C&WI	Chicago & Western Indiana		MC	Michigan Central
C&NW	Chicago & North Western		MILW	Milwaukee Road
C&O	Chesapeake & Ohio		MON	Monon
CB&Q	Chicago, Burlington & Quincy		NKP	Nickel Plate Road
CGW	Chicago Great Western		NYC	New York Central
CNS&M	Chicago, North Shore & Milwaukee		PRR	Pennsylvania
CRI&P	Chicago, Rock Island & Pacific		SC&S	South Chicago & Southern
CSS&SB	Chicago, South Shore & South Bend		SOO	Soo Line
			WAB	Wabash

See Downtown Detail Map

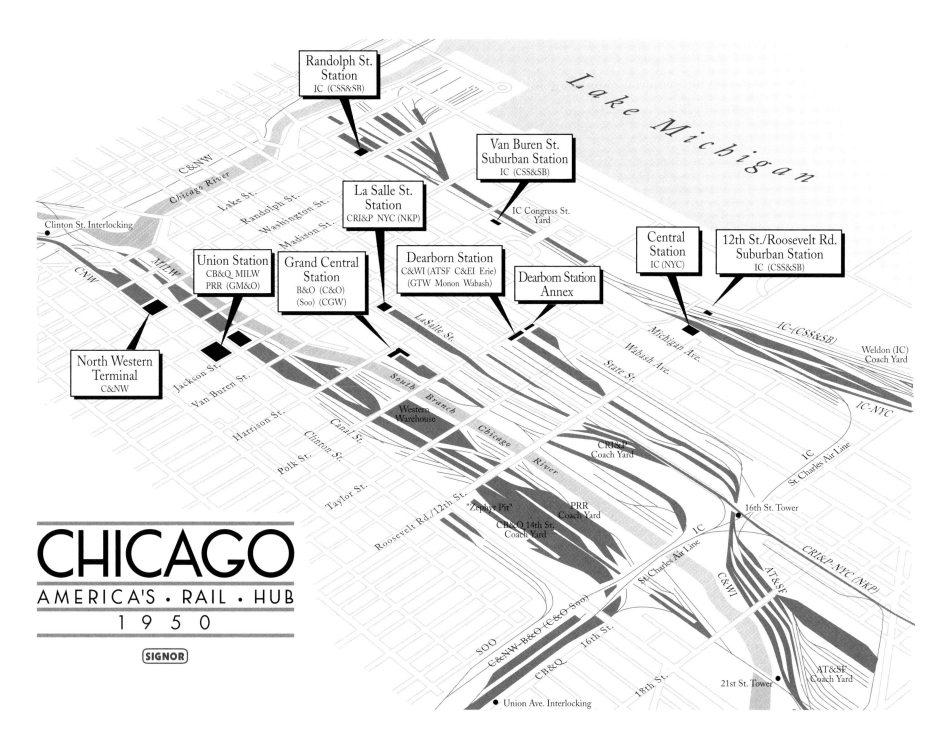

Randolph St. Station
IC (CSS&SB)

Van Buren St.
Suburban Station
IC (CSS&SB)

IC Congress St.
Yard

La Salle St.
Station
CRI&P NYC (NKP)

Central
Station
IC (NYC)

12th St./Roosevelt Rd.
Suburban Station
IC (CSS&SB)

Union Station
CB&Q MILW
PRR (GM&O)

Grand Central
Station
B&O (C&O)
(Soo) (CGW)

Dearborn Station
C&WI (ATSF C&EI Erie)
(GTW Monon Wabash)

Dearborn Station
Annex

North Western
Terminal
C&NW

Clinton St. Interlocking

C&NW

Chicago River

Lake St.

Randolph St.

Washington St.

Madison St.

CNW

MILW

Jackson St.

Van Buren St.

Harrison St.

Polk St.

Canal St.

Clinton St.

Taylor St.

LaSalle St.

South Branch

Western
Warehouse

Chicago River

State St.

Wabash Ave.

Michigan Ave.

Lake Michigan

IC-(CSS&SB)

Weldon (IC)
Coach Yard

IC-NYC

St. Charles Air Line

IC

CRI&P
Coach Yard

"Zephyr Pit"

PRR
Coach Yard

CB&Q 14th St.
Coach Yard

Roosevelt Rd./12th St.

St Charles Air Line

16th St. Tower

IC

C&WI

AT&SF

CRI&P-NYC (NKP)

SOO

C&NW-B&O (C&O Soo)

CB&Q

16th St.

18th St.

21st St. Tower

AT&SF
Coach Yard

Union Ave. Interlocking

CHICAGO
AMERICA'S · RAIL · HUB
1950

SIGNOR

11

Passenger Railroads and Stations Serving the East and South

This book looks at the railroads that provided passenger service mainly to the east and south from Chicago during the heyday of the mid-twentieth century. Twelve railroads (one of them an interurban carrier) are included. At mid-century, Chicago's passenger railroads included the powerful New York Central and Pennsylvania railroads as well as secondary carriers like the B&O and Erie. Although it provided service to St. Louis and Iowa west of Chicago, the Illinois Central is treated here because its most important trains operated from Chicago to the Deep South. The section below provides a capsule description of each of the railroads included in this volume.

Baltimore & Ohio

Baltimore & Ohio (B&O) was the first railroad in the country to offer scheduled passenger service, running its first passenger train in 1830. By the mid-twentieth century, the 6,200-mile B&O sprawled from Philadelphia to St. Louis and Chicago. The railroad's principal long-distance services were operated from Baltimore/Washington to Chicago, St. Louis, Cincinnati, and Detroit.

B&O arrived in Chicago in 1874, originally terminating at the Randolph Street Station of the Illinois Central (IC). In 1891 B&O, under a lease agreement, moved into the newly constructed Grand Central Station. By 1910 B&O had secured control of the Chicago Terminal Transfer Railroad, which became the Baltimore & Ohio Chicago Terminal Railroad (B&OCT)—a first-rate passenger and freight terminal carrier.

B&O trains accessed Grand Central via the B&OCT and the Chicago, Rock Island & Pacific. Arriving from the southeast along the shore of Lake Michigan, B&O trains entered the B&OCT at Pine Junction, Indiana, taking a leisurely course inbound to Grand Central Station, which included running on the Rock Island between Rock Island Junction and Beverly Junction. In 1969 B&O and partner Chesapeake & Ohio, operating as few as three

▶ This photo graphically illustrates Chicago & Western Indiana's role as a passenger terminal railroad. Here one of the railroad's Alco RS1s hauls equipment from both a Monon train and the C&EI's *Meadowlark* back to the C&WI coach yard at 51st Street for servicing. Wally Abbey photo

trains daily into the large facility, abandoned service into Grand Central Station. B&O/C&O then used Chicago & North Western's passenger terminal (see this book's companion volume, *Passenger Trains of Yesteryear: Chicago Westbound*) from 1969 to 1971, at which time privately operated intercity service to Chicago via the B&O ended.

Chicago & Eastern Illinois

C&EI predecessors had been operating from Dolton, Ill. (just south of Chicago), since 1872. In 1885 the C&EI commenced operation of its trains into the new Dearborn Station. The 907-mile C&EI extended from Chicago to downstate Illinois and Indiana as well as St. Louis. The road's main function as a passenger carrier was in forwarding a series of great trains to and from Florida and the South via a connection with the Louisville & Nashville at Evansville, Ind. C&EI also offered local service to the tiny hamlet of Cypress in southern Illinois.

The road's passenger service to St. Louis from Chicago succumbed to the competition of the Wabash, IC, and Gulf, Mobile & Ohio a few years after World War II. By the coming of Amtrak in 1971, C&EI route service had been scaled back to a single Chicago-Danville train—operated by the L&N, which had purchased a portion of the Chicago-Danville line.

Chicago & Western Indiana

A terminal railroad, the Chicago & Western Indiana was the idea and joint property of the predecessors of the C&EI, Wabash, Monon, Grand Trunk Western, and Erie. Creating the C&WI in the 1880s was considered easier and less expensive than having each railroad individually build lines into the city of Chicago. Chicago & Western Indiana served three main passenger purposes. First, it provided access to Dearborn Station. In addition, it served as a joint terminal company to handle the passenger cars and trains of its user roads and deliver them to the jointly used C&WI coach yard at 51st Street. (The exception was the Santa Fe, which, although it used C&WI to access Dearborn, maintained its own yard at 18th Street and switched its own cars.) Finally, the C&WI operated a limited commuter service from downtown Chicago to Dolton until August 1964. With the abandonment of Dearborn Station as a passenger terminal in May 1971, Chicago & Western Indiana's work as a passenger railroad ended.

Chicago South Shore & South Bend

The South Shore was originally completed between Hammond and South Bend, Ind., in 1908. The 91-mile line underwent a number of significant changes after Samuel Insull purchased it in 1925. Most important, the South Shore gained access to Chicago, an event that quadrupled its revenue. But the Depression and collapse of Insull's empire left the road in receivership. The road eventually recovered and, by the 1960s, despite the construction of the parallel Indiana Toll Road, service frequency was similar to that which had been offered in the boom 1920s. Passenger revenues accounted for nearly 50 percent of the line's revenues. Purchase by the C&O in 1967 led to a request by the railroad to abandon passenger service. Denied by the Interstate Commerce Commission, the effort spurred the creation of a public agency to fund lifesaving capital improvements. Today the South Shore is locally owned and is funded with public money.

South Shore trains accessed Chicago via a connection to the Illinois Central's electrified suburban lines at Kensington. CSS&SB trains used the Illinois Central from there to Randolph Street Station, where they terminate in a station next to IC's.

Erie

In the mid-1880s Erie reached Illinois over subsidiary Chicago & Atlantic Railroad, which operated from Marion, Ohio, to Hammond and via the Chicago & Western Indiana from Hammond to Chicago's Dearborn Station. Erie used Dearborn beginning in 1885. The 2,300-mile Erie operated passenger service from Jersey City (with a ferry connection to New York City) to Chicago via Elmira and Jamestown, N.Y., and Akron/Youngstown, Ohio.

In October 1960 the Erie merged with rival Delaware, Lackawanna & Western to form the new Erie Lackawanna. Neither road was a passenger powerhouse. Suffering from the competition of the PRR and NYC, which offered faster, more deluxe service to Chicago from the east, Erie Lackawanna passenger service into Chicago was but a memory by 1970.

Grand Trunk Western

The Grand Trunk Western, a Canadian National subsidiary after 1923, achieved Chicago in 1880 and began operating into Chicago's Dearborn Station in 1885 via a connection with the C&WI. Arriving from the southeast, GTW circled around to approach Chicago from the southwest and west before connecting to the C&WI at 47th Street for the ride to Dearborn.

With 1,171 miles in the United States, GTW handled trains from Port Huron and Detroit to Chicago. In conjunction with parent Canadian National, which handled the trains from Canada to Michigan, GTW offered service between Montreal, Toronto, Detroit, and Chicago and was the last railroad serving the Windy City whose intercity passenger trains were hauled by regularly assigned steam locomotives (1957).

GTW's three remaining intercity trains from Chicago survived to the advent of Amtrak, when they were discontinued.

Illinois Central

Illinois Central's entrance into Chicago, so close to the shore of

Lake Michigan, came at the instigation of the Chicago City Council in 1852. Fixing the railroad's avenue of approach to the city along the lake interposed the railroad between Michigan Avenue and Lake Michigan.

The railroad essentially traded access to Chicago for protecting the city from the ravages of the lake. Required by ordinance to maintain breakwaters, dikes, and other protection, IC saved the citizens of Chicago a considerable financial burden.

In 1853 Illinois Central constructed a station at Randolph Street and Michigan Avenue. IC opened Central Station at 11th Street in April 1893. Its intercity trains used that fashionable address near Grant Park and Michigan Avenue until the railroad exited the intercity passenger business in 1971. Befitting its status as one of Chicago's earliest railroads, IC trains reached the city via a straight, mostly grade-separated alignment from the south.

The railroad's Iowa line had a much more circuitous avenue of approach, crossing several other rail lines at grade before reaching Central Station.

IC's north-south racetrack handled the railroad's speedy trains to the south as well as the trains of

New York Central subsidiaries Michigan Central and the Big Four Route (the Cleveland, Cincinnati, Chicago & St. Louis).

The largest passenger movement over the 6,500-mile IC came not on its intercity trains but on its huge Chicago-based commuter fleet. The railroad's commuter line, electrified in 1926, extended north past Central Station about a mile to terminate at Randolph Street Station, located east of Michigan Avenue and just north of its namesake.

At mid-century, IC provided commuter service to Chicago's southern suburbs as far south as Richton Park. By the mid-1970s it would extend as far as Park Forest South. Its lines also handled the numerous daily interurban trains of the South Shore, which traveled over IC rails from Kensington/115th Street north to Randolph Street.

Although Illinois Central's distinctive chocolate- and orange-painted intercity trains disappeared with the birth of Amtrak in 1971, the IC (and South Shore) lines still provide vital public transportation for the commuters of Chicagoland.

Monon

Predecessors of the Chicago, Indianapolis & Louisville (nicknamed the Monon and renamed that officially in

the 1950s) began operating trains to Chicago from Indianapolis in 1883. In 1885 the trains began terminating at Dearborn Station.

Monon operated two lines, one linking Chicago to Indianapolis and the other from Michigan City, Ind., to Lafayette, Bloomington, French Lick, Ind., and (via a connection) to Louisville, Kentucky. The lines crossed at the hamlet of Monon, Ind., which gave the railroad its name. The railroad's 573 miles were exclusively in Indiana. It actually reached Illinois and Chicago via a connection to the C&WI at State Line Tower.

Led by the able John W. Barriger III from 1946 to 1952, the Monon dieselized and frugally added new passenger trains by rebuilding

▲ A C&WI steam switcher shuffles cars at Dearborn Station. Donald Sims photo

▶ Conductor and engineer of Erie train No. 6, the eastbound *Lake Cities,* synchronize watches shortly before departing Dearborn Station. Wally Abbey photo

surplus Army cars no longer needed after the war. In 1947, its centennial, the Monon introduced three new streamliners on a Chicago-Indianapolis daytime run and a Chicago-Louisville carding. Alas, never highly competitive, Monon's Chicago-Indianapolis service was discontinued in 1959, while the Chicago-Louisville service lasted until 1967. In July 1971 the little railroad which, had been a Hoosier favorite for 124 years, was merged with the Louisville & Nashville.

Nickel Plate Road

The New York, Chicago & St. Louis Railroad Company (nicknamed the Nickel Plate Road) began operating into Chicago in October 1882. Bouncing around between a number of stations from 1882 to 1903, the NKP finally settled in Chicago's then-new LaSalle Street Station in 1903. A key bridge route, the 2,200-mile NKP offered passenger service from Chicago to Cleveland and Buffalo, with cars for Hoboken, New Jersey (and a ferry ride to New York City), via a Lackawanna Railroad connection at Buffalo. Another key passenger route was Cleveland to St. Louis.

Despite adding streamlined cars and diesels postwar, Nickel Plate's handsome trains couldn't compete with those of the larger New York Central, the auto, or the airlines. In 1959 through-car service to New Jersey/New York City ended. In October 1964 Nickel Plate merged with the Norfolk & Western, and in September 1965 NKP's last intercity passenger trains to Chicago ceased to operate.

New York Central

One of the country's largest railroads, the New York Central first arrived in Chicago in 1852 when subsidiary Lake Shore & Michigan Southern began terminating at Clark Street, north of Roosevelt Road. In 1903 the present LaSalle Street Station was constructed, and New York Central tied up there until its trains were shifted to Union Station after the Penn Central merger.

Extending as far east as Boston at mid-twentieth century, the 10,700-mile New York Central System, an eastern giant, provided direct intercity service from Chicago to Cincinnati, Indianapolis, Cleveland, Buffalo, New York City, Boston, Detroit, and other locations. Via connections, its cars reached as far as Florida, Quebec, California, and at least a half dozen other distant termini.

New York Central's main line from New York City, Buffalo, and Cleveland entered Chicago on a fairly direct route through Gary, Ind. At Englewood it turned due north for LaSalle Street. The Michigan Central, another major NYC System route and the first railroad into Chicago from the east, terminated at IC's Central Station until 1957. It reached Central Station via its own tracks to Kensington. From there it used IC tracks into the station. In 1957 MC trains began terminating at LaSalle Street, which it reached via a connection to the New York Central Cleveland main line at Porter, Ind.

Another New York Central System route, the Big Four, offered service from IC's Central Station to Indianapolis and Cincinnati. Big Four trains traveled on the IC main line 55 miles south to Kankakee, Ill., where they entered home rails.

By 1958, in an effort to stem the red ink spreading across its ledger books, New York Central had eliminated many passenger trains. In 1968, having systematically cut back its service every year, New York Central merged with rival Pennsylvania Railroad to form Penn Central. In 1971 Penn Central entered Amtrak and ceased to provide privately funded intercity passenger service.

Pennsylvania

Direct rival to the New York Central, the mighty Pennsylvania Railroad operated its first passenger train from Chicago in September 1858 over subsidiary Pittsburgh, Fort Wayne & Chicago Railway. Another PRR subsidiary, the Pittsburgh, Cincinnati, Chicago & St. Louis ("the Panhandle") began operating into Chicago in 1861. By the early 1860s a union station serving the above roads as well as the Chicago & Alton and the Chicago, Milwaukee & St. Paul was constructed between Canal Street and the south branch of the Chicago River.

In 1880 the Pennsylvania Railroad, in cooperation with the

Chicago & Alton, the Milwaukee, and the Chicago, Burlington & Quincy, constructed a new station at the same location. That station served until it was replaced by a newer Union Station at the same site in 1925.

At mid-century, the powerful 10,000-mile Pennsylvania offered a multitude of direct passenger services from Chicago to Pittsburgh, Washington, D.C., Philadelphia, and New York City. Its distinctive Tuscan red trains also linked Chicago to Cincinnati, Indianapolis, Louisville, Florida, and, via through-car connections, to a host of other major cities.

Pennsy accessed Chicago via Gary. Just northwest of Gary its tracks ran immediately next to the New York Central as far as Englewood. There they separated but continued to parallel each other into downtown Chicago. The proximity of the two railroads and the similarity of the schedules of their top trains, the *Broadway Limited* (PRR) and the *20th Century Limited* (NYC), both destined for New York, made for one of the great spectacles in railroading as the rival trains often appeared to race each other eastbound in the afternoon.

Pennsy trains destined to the south and southeast operated through Englewood to Colehour Junction, turning onto the spindly South Chicago & Southern branch before entering the PRR's "Panhandle" main line at Bernice Junction for points south and east.

Impacted by the same economic forces that hit the New York Central, Pennsylvania reduced its passenger services severely in the 1950s. By the 1960s the railroad's service was in rapid decline, although it continued to offer a number of trains from Chicago. Pennsy merged with New York Central in 1968. On May 1, 1971, the new railroad left the intercity passenger business when Amtrak arrived. For a time, Penn Central continued to offer the modest commuter service from Chicago to Valparaiso, Ind., that Pennsy had previously operated.

Pere Marquette

Named for a French explorer and missionary, the Pere Marquette was formed in January 1900. By 1903 the railroad achieved Chicago via trackage rights from Porter, Ind., over the Lake Shore & Michigan Southern (NYC System) and the Chicago Terminal Transfer Railroad (B&O Chicago Terminal). The Pere Marquette used Grand Central Station. Primarily a Michigan-based railroad with track all over

Michigan's Lower Peninsula, the Pere Marquette provided passenger service between Chicago and Grand Rapids, Mich. It also offered service between Detroit and Grand Rapids and Toledo.

Pere Marquette route trains entered Chicago via a connection to the New York Central at Porter running on the NYC to East Chicago before cutting onto the B&OCT for the final miles into Grand Central.

In 1946 the 1,900-mile Pere Marquette began operating the first postwar lightweight streamliner of any railroad in the nation, the *Pere Marquette*. The railroad was merged into the Chesapeake & Ohio Railroad in 1947. C&O operated the line autonomously as the Pere Marquette District for several years. Parent C&O, which at first had taken an aggressively positive approach to passenger trains after World War II, reduced its efforts in the 1950s and '60s, although the Pere Marquette route trains survived until May 1, 1971, and the beginning of Amtrak.

The Stations

Befitting its status as the nation's rail hub, Chicago's eastern and southern railroads terminated at six great stations, while the interurban Chicago South Shore & South Bend tied up at the busy but nondescript

◀ Its Alco PA "Bluebird" glistening in the evening light, Nickel Plate Road's *Nickel Plate Limited* prepares to leave LaSalle Street Station. *Nickel Plate Road* magazine photo

▶ A regular event in Chicago railroading was the eastbound "race" between the PRR's *Broadway Limited* and the NYC *20th Century Limited*. Fierce competitors to New York, both trains were often scheduled out of Chicago at the same time and paced each other east from Englewood. On the left a modified Pennsy K4 has a slight lead over the *Century's* streamlined Hudson as the trains leave Englewood. Paul Eilenberger photo

Randolph Street Station. Profiled here are the five major terminals that hosted the majority of Chicago's eastern and southern intercity passenger trains. Like the railroads in the days before passenger service was nationalized, each of Chicago's major stations had a distinctive personality—a blend of its architecture, its railroads, and the people who populated the place. All of the major stations were essentially stub-end terminals, which made running trains or cars through from east to west difficult.

Dearborn Station

Oldest of Chicago's terminals, Dearborn Station was opened on May 8, 1885. Its antiquated Flemish revival headhouse (decapitated after a fire consumed its tower roof in the early part of the twentieth century) rested on Polk Street. Its ancient wooden trainshed hosted ten stub-ended tracks.

Despite being the smallest of Chicago's major terminals, tiny Dearborn was home to seven different railroads, the most of any station in Chicago. Dearborn's owner railroad was the Chicago & Western Indiana.

In the late 1940s Dearborn

handled 7,500 commuters a week on the likes of the Wabash and the C&WI, while 42,500 intercity passengers came to call. Characterized by *Trains* editor David P. Morgan as "dreary and dilapidated," Dearborn was a place one might expect to find the workaday trains of the Erie and the ancient commuter equipment of the C&WI, but never the stylish Santa Fe, whose clientele included

movie stars and moguls and whose trains ranked as some of the best in the nation. Nevertheless, thanks primarily to Santa Fe, the trains (and passengers) kept coming—until Dearborn Station closed its doors with the coming of Amtrak.

Grand Central Station

The most architecturally significant station in Chicago, marvelous

Grand Central was opened in December 1890. Designed by noted architect Solon Spencer Beman, the station was originally envisioned as a terminus for Wisconsin Central, then a subsidiary of Northern Pacific. Financial panic cut short the dream, and eventually the station (and its terminal railroad) were leased and later purchased by the B&O, giving America's first passenger railroad a stately home in Chicago.

Beman, whose other achievements include the Pullman car works buildings, designed a memorable structure. Replicating a towered Norman fortress, the station was built in an L shape. It featured a waiting room along Wells Street and a functional carriage court on Harrison Street with a semicircular-roofed train shed covering six tracks nestled in the angle formed by the two sides of the building. With an ornate interior complete with leaded stained glass, decorative iron train gates, and a marble waiting room, Grand Central fascinated the traveler with its decor.

But Grand Central's location, hard against a couple of drawbridges over the Chicago River (the river was later rerouted), made the station less convenient and reflected the difficulty of its founder road in getting access into Chicago in the first place.

At mid-century, Grand Central served owner B&O as well as Pere Marquette (C&O), Chicago Great Western, and the Minneapolis, St. Paul & Sault Ste. Marie (Soo Line). Passengers were an eclectic mix, ranging from businesspersons bound for the classy B&O Capitol Limited to campers headed for the North Woods on the Soo. With 13,000

weekly patrons in the late 1940s, all of whom were intercity passengers, Grand Central was the least used of all of Chicago's major stations—a situation that once led David P. Morgan to characterize the quiet station as the "church of Chicago railroad terminals." A victim of declining patronage and its high operating costs and real estate value, Grand Central closed its doors for good in November 1969. Its few remaining trains were moved to Chicago & North Western Terminal.

Central Station

Headquarters and terminal of the powerful Illinois Central, Central Station opened for business in April 1893. Located at Eleventh and Michigan, the station featured six through tracks under a trainshed as well as an enormous waiting room under an arched ceiling. Reflecting the Deep South influence of its owner, the station restaurant was famous for its southern cuisine. But despite its classic look and service, the station suffered from a peculiar design that forced passengers to climb a steep staircase to reach the waiting room and then descend another set of stairs to trackside.

Central was home to the wonderful trains of owner Illinois Central as well as the passenger runs of the

New York Central subsidiaries Big Four (to Cincinnati) and Michigan Central (to Detroit). In 1957 all Michigan Central trains moved to LaSalle Street Station. Conversely, in 1963 Soo Line trains started to call at Central after the Soo abandoned service to Grand Central Station.

Central Station handled approximately 31,000 passengers a week in the late 1940s. All of its customers were intercity passengers, as IC's hefty commuter business was handled at separate facilities. Serving IC trains to and from Illinois, Iowa, St. Louis, and the Deep South, Central hosted a wide variety of passengers. Among them, the elegant clientele of the swank *Panama Limited* to New Orleans, college-bound students, tourists to Florida, and the vast migration of American blacks from the rural south to the industrial cities of the north. A Chicago landmark, Central Station closed in 1972.

LaSalle Street Station

Located on the Loop in the shadow of the Chicago Board of Trade, LaSalle Street Station more resembled an office building than a big-city rail terminal. The station opened in July 1903. Its 11 stub tracks hosted the trains of owners New York Central System (NYC) and Rock Island as well as tenant

In this 1940s view toward the southeast, Illinois Central's landmark Central Station is visible in the foreground. Beyond the spire of the station is the IC coach yard. To the left are the electrified suburban tracks, which extend north to Randolph Street Station. In the distance is Soldier Field. Victor Fintak photo

Nickel Plate Road (NKP). The station also housed offices of the Rock Island, the NYC, and the NKP.

In the late 1940s, New York Central's Great Steel Fleet contributed the bulk of the station's 267,000 weekly intercity passengers, while the Rock Island conveyed the vast majority of LaSalle Street's 182,000 weekly commuters. Nickel Plate ran a solid but inconspicuous intercity service to Cleveland and Buffalo with cars for Hoboken (and New York City via a transfer to local transportation).

Inside, at street level, the station appeared to be a mere ticket office, but a ride up the escalator to the waiting room could reveal the press interviewing a famous face headed for the *20th Century Limited*. That was LaSalle Street: architecturally uninspiring but an important terminal. To this day, thanks to its handy location next to the Loop and public transportation, Chicago commuter trains still terminate in the vicinity of LaSalle Street Station, although its headhouse has been eliminated.

Union Station

Last of Chicago's major terminals constructed, Union Station was owned by the Pennsylvania, Milwaukee Road, and Burlington. Gulf, Mobile & Ohio (and its predecessor the Alton) leased space. Ironically, Milwaukee Road, which entered receivership in 1925, the year the station was opened, occupied half the terminal's tracks.

Union Station was really two buildings—one a classic Doric-columned waiting room and the other a concourse and a place to board trains. Both featured high ceilings and dramatic design—the kind of place one would expect the Pennsylvania Railroad to occupy. On the north side of the concourse, 9 stub tracks hosted the trains of the Milwaukee Road, from lowly commuters to the regal *Olympian Hiawatha* destined for Seattle and Tacoma. Starting in October 1955, Union Pacific's transcontinental trains would tie up here too. On the south side, 13 stub tracks hosted the intercity and commuter trains of the Burlington, the Pennsylvania, and the GM&O. Two through tracks on the far east side of the station permitted run-throughs or the spotting of exceptionally long trains, such as the UP/Milwaukee Domeliners.

Massive Union Station was really a small city. It included the offices of the Milwaukee Road and the Pennsylvania Railroad, a jail, an infirmary, newsstands, restaurants, and even its own police force. Union Station handled more than 190,000 commuters and 160,000 intercity passengers weekly in the late 1940s.

Between 1969 and 1971 Union's classic, glass-roofed concourse building was replaced with a misguided urban renewal project. Nevertheless, new owner Amtrak has renovated the remaining waiting room structure and revised the remaining portion of the concourse to make boarding acceptably comfortable if not the uplifting experience it was in days gone by. Today Union Station hosts all of the intercity trains terminating in Chicago, as well as a massive flow of commuters. The arrangement accomplished something no one thought possible at mid-century, when demand and internecine railroad rivalries required six different stations to handle the load.

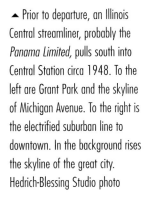

▲ Prior to departure, an Illinois Central streamliner, probably the *Panama Limited,* pulls south into Central Station circa 1948. To the left are Grant Park and the skyline of Michigan Avenue. To the right is the electrified suburban line to downtown. In the background rises the skyline of the great city. Hedrich-Blessing Studio photo

▶ To the west down Polk Street, Dearborn Station's tower rises on the left in this 1951 view. Linn Westcott photo

▲ Much of the Grand Central Station complex is visible in this 1968 shot taken from the top of the Board of Trade looking south. In the foreground are the station's Norman-style tower and trainshed. To the right is the south branch of the Chicago River. To the far left are the roof and platforms of neighbor LaSalle Street station. Richmond Bates photo

▶ This shot of the west side of Grand Central's waiting room was taken from the station's restaurant level. Phil Weibler photo

▶▶ A C&O business car on a Shriner's Special waits under the trainshed at Grand Central. The view shows off the station's stained-glass windows and ornate train gates. Phil Weibler photo

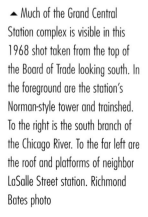

Long-Distance Trains
Serving the East and South

Hundreds of long-distance trains departed from Chicago to the east and south between the late 1800s and the 1920s. But with the rise of the automobile in the 1920s and the arrival of the Great Depression in 1929, the railroads trimmed service significantly. Despite the fact that the Depression cut ridership and revenues dramatically, eastern carriers introduced streamlined trains more slowly than their western counterparts and were also slower to embrace dieselization, another revolutionary improvement. After World War II, many new eastern streamlined trains were intro-

duced, but few carried a dome car. Clearance restrictions in the east made the dome car largely a western phenomenon. This chapter provides a snapshot of long-distance service from Chicago to the east and south circa early 1950.

Baltimore & Ohio

At mid-century, the B&O's top Chicago trains were the all-Pullman *Capitol Limited* to Washington (with cars to Jersey City and through sleepers from Los Angeles to Washington via the Santa Fe). The *Capitol* would be re-equipped with new lightweight cars, including dome sleepers, in the early 1950s. Running mate to the *Capitol* was the all-coach *Columbian*, a

dome streamliner operating between Chicago and Washington. Both the *Capitol* and the *Columbian* were considered the top trains in the Chicago-Washington market, besting the rival Pennsylvania Railroad in both schedule and service.

Secondary trains to Washington included the *Shenandoah*, the *Chicago-Pittsburgh-Washington Express* (reverse the name westbound). The *West Virginia Night Express* (*Chicago Night Express* westbound) linked the Windy City to Wheeling, West Virginia.

Chicago & Eastern Illinois

C&EI's long-distance service was oriented to the southeast. It was provided in conjunction with the

Louisville & Nashville via a connection at Evansville, Indiana. Via L&N and an alphabet soup routing of other railroads, the venerable *Dixie Flyer* offered heavyweight sleeping cars to the west coast of Florida, a dining car (on the L&N) and coaches as far south as Jacksonville. The once-posh *Dixie Limited,* formerly a through train, now offered cars to downstate Indiana— it was discontinued in 1951. On an every-third-day schedule in conjunction with trains of the Pennsylvania Railroad and the Illinois Central, the *Dixie Flagler* carried heavyweight sleepers and lightweight coaches, a diner, and tavern observation to Miami.

Beginning in 1948, the streamlined *Georgian,* previously a St. Louis-Atlanta coach train, began operating as an overnight train between Chicago, St. Louis, and Atlanta carrying heavyweight sleepers. In 1951 the streamlined *Humming Bird,* a Cincinnati-New Orleans train on the L&N, would add a Chicago leg and heavyweight sleepers as well.

Erie

Erie service to and from the east consisted of two top trains, the *Erie Limited* and the *Lake Cities* to Jersey City. Both carried some lightweight cars and were diesel powered. But neither trains' 22-plus-hour schedule was particularly competitive with New York Central's or Pennsylvania's top trains, which accomplished the same run in about 16 hours. Erie's secondary trains on the run were the *Atlantic* (or *Pacific*—westbound) *Express.*

Grand Trunk Western

Grand Trunk Western's *International Limited* offered coaches, sleeping cars, and buffet-lounge service to Toronto with a connection in parlor or coach available between Toronto and Montreal. The *LaSalle,* the *Inter-City Limited,* and the *Maple Leaf* also offered Pullman and coach service.

Illinois Central

Illinois Central's long-distance services were aimed at the Gulf Coast and Florida. To Memphis and New Orleans the all-coach streamlined *City of New Orleans* and the magnificent streamlined all-Pullman *Panama Limited* operated on fast schedules. Backstopping these flagships, the blue-collar *Louisiane* carried coaches for New Orleans and heavyweight sleepers for intermediate points. The *Southern Express* (*Northern Express* northbound) offered coaches only to New Orleans. The *Louisiane* took 24 hours to cover the same ground the flagships traveled in about 16 hours, while the *Southern Express* took a whopping 32 hours!

From Chicago to Birmingham and Florida, IC operated the daily *Seminole* and the every-third-day, streamlined *City of Miami* to the east coast of Florida. The *City* offered lightweight coaches, diners, and lounge cars, while its newly instituted sleeper service was still provided by heavyweights in early 1950. New lightweight sleepers arrived for the train later the same year. The *Seminole* provided heavyweight sleepers to the west and east coast of Florida, as well as reclining-seat coaches as far as Jacksonville.

Nickel Plate Road

The Nickel Plate offered through sleeping car and coach service to and from New York in conjunction with the Lackawanna Railroad, with which it interchanged cars at Buffalo. By spring 1950 NKP's two Chicago-Buffalo trains, the *Nickel Plate Limited* and the *Westerner* (so named westbound and unnamed eastbound), typically offered lightweight cars. But the run to Hoboken, N.J., required a ferry ride to reach Manhattan, and the fastest NKP schedule took about 21 hours.

Rivals Pennsylvania and New York Central, who accessed Manhattan directly, took an average of about 16 hours.

New York Central

Offering fast, direct, and frequent service, New York Central was one of the three principal railroads linking Chicago to the Eastern Seaboard. By 1950 its "Great Steel Fleet" had been largely re-equipped with new lightweight cars.

With fine service and sleeping and lounge cars on the tightest of schedules to and from New York, as well as two through sleepers from Los Angeles via the Santa Fe *Chief,* NYC's *20th Century Limited* was perhaps the greatest train in the nation. Backstopping the *Century* was another all-Pullman run, the *Commodore Vanderbilt.* The Budd-built, all-coach streamlined *Pacemaker* provided fast, luxurious, and affordable service to the Big Apple. A group of lesser trains with coaches and sleepers also covered the route. Some also carried through sleepers to and from the West Coast.

To Boston the principal through trains were the streamlined *New England States* and the *Interstate Express,* while a number of other secondary runs forwarded cars.

Pennsylvania

Direct rival to the New York Central in many markets, the powerful Pennsylvania operated a fleet of long-distance trains to the East Coast. Queen of the fleet was the *Broadway Limited,* all-Pullman like its competitor the *20th Century,* and also carrying a through Los Angeles sleeper to and from the *Chief.* Second to the *Broadway* on the New York-to-Chicago alignment was the all-Pullman *General,* which carried a through Los Angeles car via the Southern Pacific/Rock Island *Golden State* eastbound; it also forwarded a Los Angeles sleeper westbound to the Chicago & North Western. The all-coach streamlined *Trail Blazer* competed directly with the NYC *Pacemaker,* as it had since their joint introduction in 1939.

Other trains to New York and Philadelphia included the *Pennsylvania Limited,* the *Manhattan Limited,* the *Gotham Limited,* and the *Admiral,* many of which carried through cars to and from the West Coast.

To Washington, D.C., the streamlined *Liberty Limited* offered competing service to the B&O's *Capitol Limited* and *Columbian.* The *Manhattan Limited,* the *Pennsylvania Limited,* the *Pennsylvanian,* the *Admiral,* and the *Gotham Limited* also offered cars to or from Washington.

To Florida, via an L&N connection at Cincinnati, the PRR fielded the *Southland,* which offered heavyweight sleepers, lounges, diners, and coaches. Its two sections, one for Florida's east coast and one for the west, were merged or split at Atlanta. PRR's streamlined South Wind operated on an every-third-day schedule in cooperation with the *City of Miami* and the *Dixie Flagler.* The PRR train was forwarded over the L&N via a connection at Louisville. It carried lightweight coaches and an observation car, as well as heavyweight sleepers and a lightweight diner for Miami.

▶ B&O's *Capitol Limited* received some of the first streamlined independent diesel units in the country in 1937. In 1938 the railroad and Pullman converted existing heavy-weight cars to a modern look for the *Capitol.* They also painted them in Otto Kuhler's memorable scheme of blue and gray with gold lettering and pinstriping. Here the recently refurbished train leaves Grand Central. David P. Morgan Library collection

◀ The *Capitol Limited* carried through sleeping cars from the west after World War II. In this September 1949 shot at Grand Central, the second car in the train is a silver-painted Santa Fe 6-6-4 configuration sleeper from Los Angeles. It has been delivered by the eastbound *Chief* and is destined for Washington, D.C., Carl Bachmann photo

◄ The *Capitol Limited* is pictured departing Grand Central Station in July 1968. The cars wear traditional B&O colors, but also the yellow and blue of new partner C&O. The view towards the north provides a good look at how the station blended with the skyline of Chicago. The train's fireman leaning out of the cab door behind the engineer is about to snag a set of train orders. Phil Weibler photo

▶ Florida wasn't the only destination for an "auto train." In the summer of 1965, B&O trains Nos. 9 and 10, the *Chicago Express* and the *Washington Express,* briefly carried customers' autos on Trailer Train cars. Here train No. 9 arrives at Chicago Grand Central Station. B&O Railroad photo

▶▶ Symbolic of Chicago's role as the hub of the nation, two trains serving opposite coasts of the country meet at Dearborn Station: on the left, Santa Fe's *El Capitan* coach streamliner, just in from Los Angeles; on the right, C&EI's coach streamliner the *Dixie Flagler,* outbound for Miami. David P. Morgan Library collection

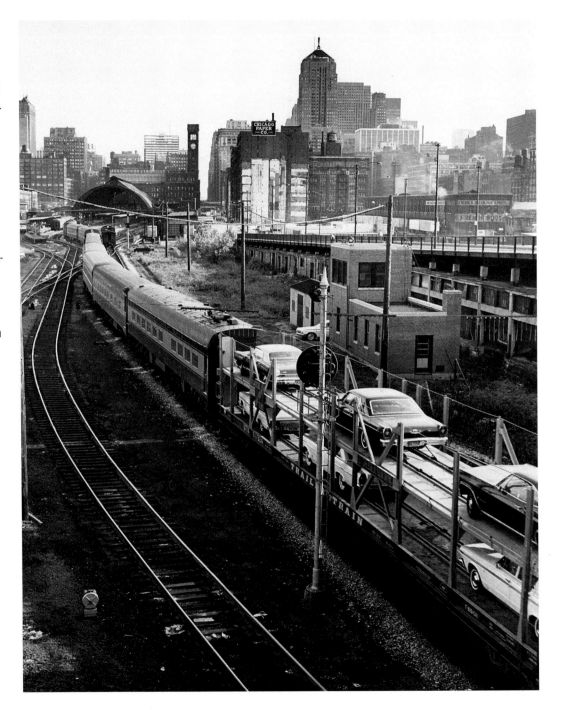

◄ With a rebuilt front end, this C&EI streamlined 4-6-2 steam locomotive has a grip on the Florida coach streamliner, the *Dixie Flagler*. Two heavyweight coaches, possibly for short-haul traffic, are inserted in the consist today. In April 1949, the train would begin handling heavyweight sleeping cars. Paul Eilenberger photo

◄ Hello, Sunshine! Behind a heavy-Pacific-type locomotive, the *Dixie Limited,* Florida bound, picks up speed as it heads south at 21st Street Junction in 1947. Just minutes out of Dearborn Station, the train is rolling over the tracks of the Chicago & Western Indiana before gaining the C&EI. The train has just swung south at the junction and is paralleling the tracks of the PRR. Donald Deneen photo

▶ A C&EI train pauses at 63rd Street, a station known as "Little Englewood," behind E7 No. 1102. William Armstrong photo

◄ Passengers prepare to board the Erle's *Lake Cities* at Dearborn Station in October 1951. Linn Westcott photo

▶ A C&WI RS1 pulls cars from the recently arrived *Erie Limited* back to the coach yard. From left to right we see Salamanca-to-Chicago 6-6-4 sleeping car "American Liberty," followed by a rebuilt heavyweight Pullman subbing for the usually assigned 10-6 lightweight. A diner-lounge is next, followed by a coach. Erie equipment in this period was painted Pullman green. The heavyweight Pullman is finished in a solid gray scheme. Wally Abbey photo

◄ Grand Trunk Western's *Maple Leaf* rolls out of Chicago behind a streamlined 4-8-4 in October 1950. GTW was the last railroad to operate intercity trains into Chicago behind steam, ending the practice in 1957. The *Maple Leaf* provided coach and Pullman service to Toronto, with through cars for Detroit connecting at Durand, Michigan. Wally Abbey photo

◄ The Grand Trunk Western's *International* for Toronto prepares to depart Dearborn Station in July 1968. Two CN sleepers, one a "Val"-series 22-roomette car, precede the B&O's "Mahoning," which contains 14 roomettes and 4 double bedrooms. Richmond Bates photo

◄ Standard steam also pulled GTW's trains to and from Chicago. Here the *Maple Leaf* departs Dearborn Station behind a 4-8-4 in June 1949. Charles McCreary photo

▶ Grand Trunk Western's outbound *Maple Leaf,* powered by two GP9s, is pictured at 21st Street on its last run from Chicago in May 1971. Burdell L. Bulgrin photo

▶ Grand Trunk Western train No. 20, the *Maple Leaf,* leaves Dearborn Station behind a classic 4-8-4 in August 1955. Jim Scribbins photo

◀ Grand Trunk Western train No. 20, the *Maple Leaf,* behind 4-8-4 No. 6405, steams out of Chicago at the 21st Street tower. The date: October 4, 1950. Wally Abbey photo

▸ The heavyweight *Panama Limited* prepares to depart Central Station on its fast run to New Orleans. Lightweight equipment is just around the corner. Richard Luryman photo

▸▸ The brand new *City of New Orleans* on the left and an unidentified intercity train (right) flank two Illinois Central suburban trains at 35th Street in Chicago in 1947. The shot is a posed publicity piece, but IC long-distance trains ran parallel to the electrics like this every day on the railroad's wide right-of-way south of downtown. IC photo

▶ First re-equipped as a light-weight in 1942, the *Panama Limited* was upgraded again in 1950. In 1953 new 11-double-bedroom sleepers arrived. This shot shows the train post-1953 along-side Chicago's Grant Park. IC trains were kept spotless, and the glistening new flagship is no exception. IC photo

▶▶ The blue-collar *Louisiane,* carrying coaches for New Orleans and heavyweight sleepers for intermediate points, prepares to depart Central Station at twilight. Bruce Meyer photo

▶ The very last Illinois Central *Panama Limited* ever to depart Chicago passes the IC coach yard outbound from Central Station. It's April 30th, 1971, and tomorrow what's left of the nation's passenger trains will be run by Amtrak. The *Panama,* which has been one of the nation's greatest trains since 1911, will be discontinued. Harold Edmondson photo

▶ Nickel Plate Road's premier train from Cleveland and New York, the *Nickel Plate Limited,* is pictured leaving Englewood northbound for LaSalle Street in 1936 behind one of the road's Hudsons. D. W. Yungmeyer photo

▲ Toward the end of its life, a
Nickel Plate Hudson hauls train No.
8 out of LaSalle Street in March
1955. The Hudsons sometimes
subbed for Alco PAs, which had
arrived on the property in 1947
and 1948. Jim Scribbins photo

▶ Nickel Plate PA diesels have a grip on No. 7, the *Westerner,* arriving at Englewood in August 1948. Bob Borcherding photo

▶ On what may be its first run as a streamlined train (June 15, 1938), the *20th Century Limited* departs LaSalle Street Station. The sleek Hudson, styled by the legendary Henry Dreyfuss, will eventually become a symbol of the streamlined era. Alexander Maxwell photo

▶ Wearing its second prewar streamlined paint scheme, a Hudson rolls east from Englewood with the *20th Century Limited*. Richard J. Cook photo

◀ Streamlined Hudson 5452 with a long-distance tender heads the *Century* eastbound at Englewood. Later in its career, this locomotive suffered a boiler explosion. Paul Eilenberger photo

▶ New York Central dieselized the *20th Century* and other top trains shortly after World War II. Champing at the bit and ready to run, shiny new E7s idle on the head end of the crack train, pictured here waiting to depart LaSalle Street Station in 1946. NYC photo

▸ Snow, the bane of airlines and motorists, wreaked havoc on the railroads, too. The snow belt near the Great Lakes was especially challenging. In this terrific shot, New York Central's westbound *Water Level Limited* enters Englewood two hours late behind a Niagara 4-8-4 in January 1947. Milton B. Nafus photo

▸▸ Niagara No. 6007 rolls out of LaSalle Street Station with train No. 28, the *New England States,* on October 20, 1950. The train operated via Cleveland and Buffalo to Boston. Bob Borcherding photo

► F3s are power—unusual for New York Central, which relied mostly on E units. The photo was taken from Roosevelt Road looking north in the afternoon. David P. Morgan Library collection

▲ Looking south from Roosevelt Road around 5 p.m., we see the *20th Century Limited* departing on the left and Rock Island suburban trains waiting to the right. The year is 1947 or '48, and the *Century's* consist and paint scheme are in transition. Ed Kriss photo

◀ Long trains sometimes taxed the length of LaSalle Street's platforms. Here passengers detrain from New York Central's *New England States* well beyond the station's platform canopy. A redcap walks toward the rear of the train, a porter wipes down the handrails to his car, and a passenger gives the photographer the once-over before heading into the station. Wally Abbey photo

◄◄ Second only to the *Century* in prestige, New York Central's all-Pullman *Commodore Vanderbilt* is seen here eastbound in 1949 behind Alco PAs at the Clark Street interlocking. The train is crossing the St. Charles Air Line, which allowed IC Iowa line trains to cross town east-west from Central Station. Donald Sims photo

◄ A rebuilt "Island"-series observation car, originally assigned to the *20th Century Limited,* carries the drumhead of the *Commodore Vanderbilt* as it pauses at Englewood westbound in April 1948. Bob Borcherding photo

▶ In the boom years of the 1920s, the NYC's *20th Century Limited* often ran in multiple sections to accommodate demand. On a snowy day in the early part of the decade, five sections of the *Century* prepare to depart LaSalle Street Station. NYC photo

◀ A New York Central flyer passes the tower at the TP&W crossing in Sheldon, Illinois, on the line to Danville, Ill. The air-conditioning ducts on the roofs of the railroad cars indicate that the shot was taken after the mid 1930s. David P. Morgan Library collection

▶ The New York Central *20th Century Limited,* perhaps the greatest train in the world, is shown at the height of its popularity in the heavyweight era of the 1920s. It is pulled by a classic Hudson steam locomotive and has just cleared the Calumet River on its run into Chicago. David P. Morgan Library collection

As seen from the Pennsylvania Railroad right-of-way, a streamlined Hudson with a long-distance tender has a roll on an NYC train near 82nd and South Chicago Avenue in April 1946. David P. Morgan Library collection

◄ The PRR's *Broadway Limited* was photographed on its inaugural eastbound run as a streamliner on June 15, 1938. K4 locomotive No. 3768, elegantly streamlined by Raymond Loewy, hauls the Tuscan red streamliner. Vernon Seaver photo

◄ About five miles southeast of Englewood on the far south side of Chicago, the New York Central and Pennsylvania crossed the Calumet River on these impressive bridges. This NYC train is eastbound. John Crosby photo

▶ Pennsylvania experimented with its S1 steam locomotive. Measuring more than 140 feet in length and weighing more than a million pounds, No. 6100 had a unique 6-4-4-6 wheel arrangement. Alas, the "Big Engine's" gorgeous design couldn't help its engineering short-comings. Nevertheless, the one-of-a-kind giant No. 6100 routinely handled PRR varnish on the west end of the railroad. Here it hauls the eastbound *Manhattan Limited* through Englewood in November 1939. Harold Stirton photo

◄ Introduced in July 1939, Pennsy's all-coach streamliner, the *Trail Blazer,* between Chicago and New York was phenomenally successful before World War II. The eastbound train is seen boarding at Englewood. The little boy on the platform keeps a sharp eye on the crew tending to K4 No. 5471. Train name signs, a PRR tradition, routinely identified the road's top varnish. PRR photo

▶ In March 1949, a PRR K4 accelerates past the railroad's coach yard south of Union Station with a Pennsy long-distance train in tow. G. E. Lloyd photo

▶ PRR T1 No. 5507 pulls the eastbound *Broadway Limited* at 22nd Street in Chicago. PRR rostered 52 of the Loewy-styled 4-4-4-4 steamers, which were displaced in their prime by diesels. Wally Abbey photo

▶ In March 1948, the eastbound *Manhattan Limited* crosses the Chicago River South Branch lift bridge at 21st Street en route to New York behind a stylish T1. Robert Milner photo

▶▶ A *Trail Blazer* sandwich: (left) locomotive No. 5514, a T1 inbound with train 215/315 from Indianapolis and Louisville, and (right) M1 locomotive No. 6975, with a westbound freight train, pass the observation car of PRR's eastbound *Trail Blazer* at Englewood in July 1947. Milton B. Nafus photo

◄ Pennsy's *South Wind* was a coach streamliner between Chicago and Florida. Inaugurated in December 1940, the seven-car lightweight train was delivered by the Budd Company and finished in PRR's traditional Tuscan red. Sometime before April 1949, the train is pictured southbound on 21st Street behind a decidedly unstreamlined K4 locomotive. Milton B. Nafus photo

▲ It's a little before 5 p.m., and a Union Station gateman checks his watch while a fellow employee makes the last boarding call announcement for Pennsylvania's all-Pullman *Broadway Limited*. Through gate 24 lies 15½ hours of pampering en route to New York on what some called the finest train in the country. Mel Patrick photo

◄◄ Cream of the Pennsy fleet, the all-Pullman *Broadway Limited* flies eastward to Philadelphia and New York, shortly after being re-equipped in 1949. PRR photo

◄ The newly re-equipped all-Pullman *Broadway Limited,* just in from New York, is headed for Union Station in October of 1950. Wally Abbey photo

Medium-Distance Trains
Midwest Favorites

A variety of shorter-distance rail passenger routes linked Chicago and major cities to the east and south. Between Chicago and St. Louis, Illinois Central offered three trains daily in competition with the GM&O (Alton) and the Wabash, while C&EI had recently bowed out of the race. From Chicago to Detroit the New York Central competed with the Grand Trunk Western. Rival Pennsy's *Detroit Arrow* and *Chicago Arrow* had ceased operation in 1949. To Cincinnati, New York Central offered up to five trains, while PRR fielded four trains. Chicago to Indianapolis and Louisville saw the competition of the PRR (four trains), Monon (two trains to Indianapolis, one to Louisville), and the NYC (six trains as far as Indianapolis, five on their way to Cincinnati). Pere Marquette offered the sole service to Grand Rapids, Michigan.

Other, less obvious markets also existed. For a brief period, C&EI fielded two relatively unknown streamliners—one terminating in the rural southern Illinois hamlet of Cypress and the other terminating in Evansville, Ind. In addition to its high-profile streamliners to the southland via Memphis, Tennessee, Illinois Central also offered three trains daily on its Iowa line as far as Sioux City, Iowa.

This chapter sums up the services offered as of mid-century.

Chicago & Eastern Illinois

C&EI operated two relatively obscure medium-distance streamliners. From Chicago to Evansville, Ind., the *Whippoorwill* was a short-lived day train that was introduced in 1946 and withdrawn in 1951. From Chicago to downstate Illinois at Cypress (population 300), C&EI ran the *Meadowlark* until it was replaced by a Rail Diesel Car in the mid-1950s. Both trains were attired in C&EI's attractive blue-and-orange paint scheme. To Danville, Ill., went unnamed trains 15 and 16.

81

Illinois Central

Illinois Central's *Green Diamond* to and from St. Louis had been introduced in 1936 as a unique streamlined train set painted in distinctive shades of green. By the late 1940s, the train had been re-equipped with new lightweight cars attired in traditional chocolate and orange. Its daytime running mate, the *Daylight*, was also similarly upgraded. On the overnight run, the *Night Diamond* carried heavyweight sleepers and coaches, including one sleeping car that was set out en route at the state capital of Springfield. For a time this Pullman car line was operated on an alternating basis, carried one month on the Illinois Central and the other on the competing GM&O.

On its western line across Iowa, the IC offered three trains daily. The *Hawkeye*, with heavyweight sleepers, coaches, and a buffet lounge, covered the overnight card-ing to Sioux City. The streamlined *Land O' Corn* to and from Waterloo, Iowa, offered reclining-seat coaches, a cafe lounge, and westbound dining-car service (as far as Freeport, Ill.). The daytime *Iowan* with coaches and a cafe lounge went as far as Fort Dodge.

Monon

In 1947 and 1948 the Monon introduced three streamlined trains. The cars, rebuilt from new surplus Army equipment, upgraded the venerable *Hoosier* between Chicago and Indianapolis and created the *Tippecanoe* between Chicago and Indianapolis and the *Thoroughbred* between Chicago and Louisville. The bright little streamliners were originally attired in crimson, gray, and white to honor home-state Indiana University at Bloomington. Between Chicago and Bloomington, to handle the college trade, the railroad also intermittently operated the *Varsity*, a coach train.

New York Central

The streamlined *Twilight Limited* and *Chicago Mercury* were run by the Michigan Central and operated to Detroit out of Central Station in Chicago. The *Mercury* had been the first streamliner on the route in 1939. Overnight, the *Motor City Special* offered lightweight and heavyweight sleeping cars and coaches. Unlike its brethren, the *Wolverine*, destined for Detroit and New York, left from LaSalle Street Station. Central's Detroit trains competed directly with Grand Trunk Western, which offered service to Detroit.

To Indianapolis and Cincinnati, New York Central subsidiary Big Four offered six trains per day, including the eastbound *Carolina Special*, which carried sleepers destined for the Southern Railway at

Cincinnati and the Carolinas. Only going as far as Indianapolis was the *Indianapolis Mail,* an all-stops local (its closest westbound counterpart was the *Chicago Special*). The top train on the run was the daytime *James Whitcomb Riley* (named for the Indiana poet) originally streamlined in 1941 and largely re-equipped in the late 1940s. The *Cincinnati Night Express* (*Chicago Night Express* westbound) covered the overnight run with sleeping cars and coaches. Westbound, the workingman's *Sycamore* and the *White City Special* also offered service. Numerous Central trains served Cleveland in competition with the Nickel Plate, which offered service through Cleveland as far as Buffalo.

Pennsylvania

From Chicago covering all stops, PRR offered the *Union*, a daytime run to Cincinnati with sleeping cars all the way to Norfolk via a connec-tion to the N&W at the Queen City. On its way to and from Florida, the long-distance train the *Southland* provided a lightweight sleeper to Cincinnati on the overnight run. Two other unnamed train pairs (Nos. 215/216 daytime and Nos. 236/237 overnight) also covered the run with train No. 215 handling the westbound Norfolk-Chicago sleeper the *Union* carried eastbound.

Indianapolis and Louisville received overnight service via the *Kentuckian* with lightweight and heavyweight sleepers. The Florida bound streamliner the *South Wind* offered daytime service. Via a shuffle at Logansport, Indiana, sections of the *Union* forwarded cars to Indianapolis and Louisville as well as Cincinnati and Columbus. Columbus was also served by the overnight *Ohioan* and the daytime *Fort Hayes.* Nameless trains 115/315 and 116/316 offered a parlor cafe car and coaches on the daytime run between Chicago and Louisville.

To Pittsburgh went the overnight *Golden Triangle* and the daytime *Fort Pitt.*

Pere Marquette (Chesapeake & Ohio)

Trains Nos. 2 and 7 provided overnight sleeping-car service and coaches between Chicago and Grand Rapids. Trains Nos. 5 and 8 were streamliners on the daytime run. Each streamliner was robed in *Pere Marquette's* distinctive maize-and-blue scheme and offered a tavern-diner, coaches, and snack service. Later they would briefly receive dome cars. C&O acquired the Pere Marquette in 1947.

84

On C&WI trackage, C&EI's *Zipper* crosses the PRR at 21st Street. One hundred forty-five miles out of Chicago, the St. Louis-bound train will connect at Villa Grove with a railcar destined for the region in southern Illinois known as Egypt with town names like Karnak and Thebes. The connecting railcar run was named the *Egyptian Zipper*, perhaps the oddest train name in North America. Rail Photo Service photo

◄ C&EI's *Zipper* prepares to depart Dearborn Station for St. Louis. Workers tinkering with frozen switches and the steam rising from locomotives leave no doubt that Chicago is in the grip of Old Man Winter. Rail Photo Service photo

◄◄ C&EI's obscure blue-and-orange streamliner, the *Meadowlark*, pictured here southbound at C&WI's 63rd Street Station, called by many "Little Englewood" (a comparison with the PRR-NYC-RI Englewood to the east). The *Meadowlark* terminated at the unlikely location of Cypress, Ill. (population 300). William N. Clark photo

◄ The *Meadowlark* heads inbound to Dearborn Station at 21st Street. On the rear end is C&EI office car "Danville." The two fluted-side cars in the consist formerly belonged to the Pere Marquette. Wally Abbey photo

◄ On a warm August evening in 1946, three heavyweight Pullmans wait for passengers in Chicago's Central Station. The train is probably the *Night Diamond* to St. Louis, but the time (11:00 p.m.) and the consist make absolute identification difficult. Curtis Thatcher photo

▲ The *Green Diamond* of 1936 was Illinois Central's first streamliner. Finished in a two-tone green scheme, the train operated on a daytime schedule between Chicago and St. Louis. It is pictured here en route to Central Station south of 47th Street in Chicago. Philip Korst, Jr. photo

◄ IC's streamliner *Land O' Corn* from Waterloo, Iowa, is eastbound about 15 miles from Chicago. The train offered reclining-seat coaches and a cafe lounge. Bob Borcherding photo

▼ Before being streamlined, the Monon's *Hoosier* is pictured southbound at 47th Street. Rail Photo Service photo

◄ Not all IC trains were streamliners or heavyweight Pullman runs. The blue-collar *Sinnissippi* with coaches from Chicago to Freeport, Ill., is pictured outbound at 21st Street in 1947. Milton B. Nafus photo

▶ The Monon *Tippecanoe* for Indianapolis is on the roll bucking the morning inbound rush. On the left, a Santa Fe overnight train has arrived, while on the right a Grand Trunk Western train is docking. A Santa Fe switcher removes other cars from the station. Harold E. Williams photo

▶ Monon's outbound *Tippecanoe* approaches 21st Street in 1950 behind two red-and-gray F3s. Wally Abbey photo

▶ With an RPO, two reclining-seat coaches, and a parlor grill car, the last three from rebuilt Army hospital cars, the *Tippecanoe* departs Chicago for Indianapolis in 1950. The train has just cleared the diamonds of 21st Street. Wally Abbey photo

▲ Trains of NYC subsidiary
Michigan Central generally used
IC's Central Station. Here the
Chicago Mercury prepares to depart
on its morning-to-mid-afternoon run
to Detroit. Richard Luryman photo

At the beginning of the stream-lined era, solid heavyweight trains were the norm rather than the exception. Michigan Central's *Twilight Limited* with coaches, parlor cars, and dining service for Detroit typifies the breed. The train is pictured racing southbound on the Illinois Central at 95th Street in August 1936 behind a magnificent 4-6-4 Hudson. D. W. Yungmeyer photo

Departing Central Station for Detroit in late afternoon behind an Alco PA/PB set, the *Twilight Limited* of 1951 was a member in good standing of New York Central/Michigan Central's Great Steel Fleet of streamliners. Bob Borcherding photo

◄◄ Never as cosmopolitan as some of Chicago's other stations, which offered seemingly limitless variety, Central Station puts on a good show in this photograph. From left to right, we see IC's *Panama Limited,* Michigan Central's *Twilight Limited,* and IC's *Seminole* (with Central of Georgia power) for Florida. Bob Borcherding photo

◄ Michigan Central's *Motor City Special* offered lightweight and heavyweight sleeping cars and coaches overnight on the Chicago-Detroit run. The eastbound train is pictured pulling away from Illinois Central's Kensington-115th Street Station, entering MC trackage. MC was the first railroad to reach Chicago from the east, using IC from Kensington into the city. A. C. Kalmbach photo

▶ Pennsylvania's *Union,* a daytime run to Cincinnati with sleeping cars all the way to Norfolk via the Norfolk & Western, departs Chicago in October 1950 behind two massive Baldwin "Centipede" diesels. On the right is the PRR's coach yard; on the left in the rear, pacing the train, is the CB&Q/Great Northern *Empire Builder,* bound for the Pacific Northwest. Bob Borcherding photo

▶ A Pennsy K4 rumbles over the 21st Street Junction with a Louisville train as a track section crew watches. It's March 1951, and the PRR is rapidly replacing its aging steam fleet with shiny new diesels. Robert Milner photo

◄ Englewood, southeast of Chicago, was an important junction and station. Englewood Union Station handled the trains of the NYC, PRR, Rock Island, and Nickel Plate. Here the PRR's *Cincinnati Daylight Express* heads east across the Rock Island before entering the station. Eastbound New York Central trains angled into the station from the far left using the station platforms seen beyond the peaked-roof depot building. PRR photo

▲ PRR's Chicago-Fort Wayne-Detroit *Detroit Arrow* pulls out of Englewood. This train and its westbound counterpart, the *Chicago Arrow,* were discontinued in September 1949. They rode Wabash rails between Fort Wayne and the Motor City. David P. Morgan Library collection

▸ The C&O Pere Marquette division's daytime trains between Chicago and Grand Rapids were robed in PM's distinctive maize-and-blue scheme. They offered a tavern-diner, coaches, and snack service. Train No. 8 is pictured outbound to Grand Rapids at Western Avenue Junction (north of the CB&Q) in July 1949. This photo and the one on the opposite page are coming and going views of the same train. Robert Milner photo

▸▸In this fine going-away shot, Pere Marquette train No. 8 is made up of equipment from the road's original streamlined order as well as cars from parent C&O's stillborn Chessie streamliner, including a dome observation car still adorned with "Chessie's" profile. Bob

Chicago's Commuter Trains

▶ South Shore's 1926-built fleet continued in service until 1983. One year before its retirement, passengers board a timeworn South Shore car at Michigan City, Indiana. Kevin Scanlon photo

Five of Chicago's "eastern" railroads provided commuter rail service. Of these the most important was the Illinois Central, whose massive fleet of electrified trains handled more passengers than any other railroad serving the Windy City. But the grouping also included one high-volume interurban and a little-known railroad whose tiny commuter service existed in the shadows of the giants. The following is a brief summary of commuter rail operations at mid-century.

Chicago South Shore & South Bend

South Shore's real contribution as a Chicago-area commuter carrier began in 1926, when the interurban line underwent significant upgrades and the railroad began receiving a fleet of new cars. In the same year the railroad gained trackage rights over the newly electrified Illinois Central commuter line to Randolph Street Station in the heart of downtown. As a result, ridership increased dramatically until 1929, when it was negatively impacted by the Depression. The unprecedented demand of World War II caused a rebound in traffic.

During and after the war the railroad modernized 36 of its cars, lengthening them to increase capacity. The 1926 fleet would continue in service until 1983. In the late 1940s the South Shore operated approximately 66 trains. Many of the runs extended as far as South Bend, Ind., while some services extended only as far east as Gary/Tremont or Michigan City, Ind.

The introduction of the parallel Indiana Toll Road in the late 1950s and the C&O's purchase of the railroad in 1967 resulted in declines in passenger traffic and a request to cut service. In 1972 the railroad reduced the number of trains it operated, but its request for complete discontinuance in 1976, coupled with a recognition of the importance of the commuter rail line, spurred the creation of a public agency to operate the vital service, which continues today.

Chicago & Western Indiana

C&WI operated a limited commuter service from Chicago south 16.6 miles to and from Dolton. Hauled originally by steam Moguls and later by Alco RS-1 diesels, its ancient fleet of Stillwell cars and a round-roof combine called at a series of quaint gingerbread-style wood-frame stations. On August 28, 1964, the obscure commuter service, which had changed little since the steam era, was discontinued.

Illinois Central

Illinois Central operated its first commuter train to Chicago in 1856. Before long the railroad expanded the operation to provide the most extensive suburban service of any railroad serving Chicago. In 1926 the railroad electrified its commuter lines. Its fleet of 130 dark green motor cars and 130 (unpowered) trailer cars terminated and originated at Chicago's Randolph Street Station, which had an adjacent facility for trains of the CSS&SB.

IC's commuter service was provided under electric overhead catenary on three routes. A double-track electrified branch line served south Chicago; a single-track electric branch (with a passing siding) extended to Blue Island. The main commuter line was made up of three tracks from Randolph Street to 11th Place, six tracks between 11th Place and 51st Street, four tracks from 51st Street to Kensington, and two tracks from Kensington to Richton Park. In modern

▶ An eastbound CSS&SB train pauses at the East Chicago Station in August 1946. H. A. List photo

times a single-track extension reached from Richton Park to Park Forest South, now University Park.

In the late 1940s, IC operated 416 express and local commuter trains per day into and out of Randolph Street Station, and the railroad handled an amazing 175,000 passenger trips per day. The view of a fast-moving commuter train being passed by an even faster-moving IC streamliner on the road's multiple-track line was one of the great sights in American railroading.

Publicly funded commuter trains still operate today over the IC electric lines, providing a vital service.

New York Central

As of 1950, New York Central offered a moderate commuter service between Chicago and Porter, Chesterton and La Porte, Ind., and a limited service as far east as Elkhart, Ind. While much of the service was curtailed in the 1950s, the last runs to Elkhart survived until 1964.

Pennsylvania

Circa 1950, Pennsylvania offered two inbound commuter runs, nick-named "Dummies," to Chicago from Valparaiso, Ind., in the morning and two outbound runs in the afternoon. The railroad continued the same service through its merger as Penn Central. Eventually the service was taken over by Amtrak before being discontinued.

▲ An outbound Chicago South
Shore & South Bend train is at IC's
Roosevelt Road suburban station,
adjacent to Central Station, in this
view taken in April 1949. Donald
Sims photo

▲ A steam-hauled Chicago & Western Indiana suburban train leaves Englewood for Dolton, Ill., in August 1947. Robert Milner photo

▶ Train No. 75, the C&WI's commuter run from Dolton to Chicago, is pictured on its last run on August 28, 1964, with an Alco RS1 towing three Stillwell coaches. Burdell L. Bulgrin photo

113

▶ Commuters stream off an IC suburban train at Van Buren Street. IC handled more commuters than any other Chicago railroad. A. C. Kalmbach photo

▶▶ Commuting on the IC in 1895: six steam-hauled suburban trains are prepared to head southbound from the Randolph Street passenger station. IC photo

▲ IC eventually electrified its suburban service routes. On August 7, 1926, four brand-new electric suburban trains are decorated for the inauguration of service. IC photo

◄ Passengers board an IC Washington Park racetrack special at Kensington station. Racetrack specials, which used a now-abandoned branch from Harvey to the racetrack, were common and often operated on headways as tight as 10 minutes. William D. Middleton photo

▶ A midday South Chicago
Express leaves Randolph Street
Station in August 1956. In the
right background is the Prudential
Building, which occupies air rights
over the station. William D.
Middleton photo

◀ Graphically illustrating that both IC and CSS&SB shared IC track and Randolph Street Station access, an IC train arrives while a South Shore train is being switched. William D. Middleton photo

119

◄ A long string of IC electric m.u. cars in multiple-track territory around 53rd Street symbolizes the typical IC suburban train. IC photo

▲ A view looking north toward the skyline of Chicago shows IC suburban electric cars stored at the 18th Street Multiple Unit Shop. Soldier Field is in the background to the right. Southbound electrics used the tracks in foreground; northbounds the tracks at right. David P. Morgan Library collection

◄ Pennsylvania Railroad suburban train at Englewood station about to depart outbound to Valparaiso, Ind., on April 12, 1941. D.W. Yungmeyer photo.

▲ John Gruber took this photo from the Harrison Street tower on July 24, 1964. The heavyweight is part of the Pennsy commuter train outbound to Valparaiso, Ind.

Chicago's Passenger Trains Today

▶ An Amtrak train leaving Chicago Union Station in September 1997 passes 14th Street, the former Pennsylvania Railroad facility that now serves as Amtrak's Chicago car and locomotive maintenance and servicing base. Robert S. McGonigal photo

Chicago remains the nation's rail passenger hub today. And some things have stayed the same. On a typical weekday more than 650 commuter trains come and go on 13 different lines. Today, most are operated by Metra, a regional rail transportation provider. Trains on the South Shore Line are operated by the Northern Indiana Commuter Transportation District.

As in the past, the Illinois Central route generates the greatest commuter ridership and is served by the largest number of trains. But the former Burlington Route Aurora line is heavily used, as are the former C&NW, Milwaukee Road, and Rock Island routes. The former Wabash line to Orland Park also carries commuters, although on far fewer trains than the others.

Commuter trains still terminate at Union Station, North Western Terminal (its classic headhouse has been replaced by a skyscraper), LaSalle Street Station, and Randolph Street Station.

But some things have changed. IC's Central Station is gone. Wonderful Grand Central Station, the most architecturally significant terminal in the city's history (closed in part for its real estate value) is gone. Much of the land where the station once stood is, ironically, still vacant. Dearborn Station's facade survives, but trains don't terminate at the old facility.

In addition to the stations, the greatest change has come to the intercity fleet. Hundreds of intercity passenger trains operated by numerous private railroads once called Chicago home. Today the number of intercity trains operating into and out of Chicago has dropped to about 50 per day. They all terminate at Union Station and are all operated by Amtrak. The fleet is relatively homogeneous in appearance, with trains sporting Amtrak's red, white, and blue scheme. With intercity trains all run by one carrier through one terminal, operating efficiencies have been applied to save time and money. For example, the arriving

City of New Orleans trainset departs later the same day than the *Empire Builder,* and vice versa.

A look in the timetable reveals that some of the great names have vanished. Chicago no longer hosts a *Super Chief,* a *Broadway Limited,* a *20th Century Limited,* a *Panama Limited* or a *City* fleet destined for the West Coast. But, a surprising number of the great names remain—although the services offered, and in some cases the routes themselves, have changed. A *Capitol Limited* still links Chicago and Washington, D.C. Passengers can board the *California Zephyr* and travel through the spectacular Colorado Rockies en route to the Bay Area. The *Empire Builder* still links Chicago to the Pacific Northwest. A *Hiawatha* fleet continues to operate to Milwaukee (albeit as a virtual commuter train) and a *Chief* (*Southwest Chief*) still connects Chicago to Los Angeles, traveling through the deserts of the southwest.

Though rail passenger service into and out of Chicago is greatly reduced from what it was during the Golden Years, Chicago is still a highly significant rail hub. The call of "All Aboard" will most likely beckon passengers in the Windy City for a long time to come.

Index of Photographs